CELEBRATING THE CITY OF BOGOTA

Celebrating the City of Bogota

Walter the Educator

Silent King Books
A WhichHead Entertainment Imprint

Copyright © 2024 by Walter the Educator

All rights reserved. No part of this book may be reproduced in any manner whatsoever without written per- mission except in the case of brief quotations embodied in critical articles and reviews.

First Printing, 2024

Disclaimer

This book is a literary work; the story is not about specific persons, locations, situations, and/or circumstances unless mentioned in a historical context. Any resemblance to real persons, locations, situations, and/or circumstances is coincidental. This book is for entertainment and informational purposes only. The author and publisher offer this information without warranties expressed or implied. No matter the grounds, neither the author nor the publisher will be accountable for any losses, injuries, or other damages caused by the reader's use of this book. The use of this book acknowledges an understanding and acceptance of this disclaimer.

Celebrating the City of Bogota is a little collectible souvenir book that belongs to the Celebrating Cities Book Series by Walter the Educator. Collect them all and more books at WaltertheEducator.com

USE THE EXTRA SPACE TO TAKE NOTES AND DOCUMENT YOUR MEMORIES

BOGOTA

In Bogotá, where dawn paints skies with gold,

Celebrating the City of Bogota

A city of stories, ancient and bold.

Nestled high in the Andean crest,

Its vibrant heart knows no rest.

Mountains embrace this spirited land,

Where myths and modernity hand in hand.

Streets alive with whispers of old,

In every corner, tales unfold.

El Dorado's echoes in the air,

Legends of gold, everywhere.

Markets hum with life's embrace,

In every smile, a hidden grace.

Candelaria, with its cobblestone ways,

Houses history, art, and sunlit days.

Mosaics of color, murals profound,

In Bogotá, beauty is all around.
Celebrating the City of Bogota

La Séptima pulses with the beat,

Of dreams, of hopes, of every street.

From Usaquén's charm to Teusaquillo's sprawl,

In Bogotá, the spirit stands tall.

And the ciclovía, a river of wheels,

Celebrating the City of Bogota

Where the city moves, and freedom feels.

Bikes and laughter fill the air,

In Bogotá, there's life everywhere.

Monserrate's peak watches all,

A guardian ancient, standing tall.

Pilgrims climb with hearts in hand,

To touch the sky, to understand.

The city's breath, a rhythmic sound,

With every pulse, connections found.

Libraries of wisdom, universities' light,

Celebrating the City of Bogota

In Bogotá, knowledge takes flight.

Parque Simón Bolívar's green embrace,

A respite in the city's race.

Here, families gather, friends unite,

Under the stars, dreams take flight.

Gastronomic treasures, a feast for the soul,

Ajiaco, arepas, stories untold.

In every dish, a blend of past,

In Bogotá, flavors unsurpassed.

ABOUT THE CREATOR

Walter the Educator is one of the pseudonyms for Walter Anderson. Formally educated in Chemistry, Business, and Education, he is an educator, an author, a diverse entrepreneur, and he is the son of a disabled war veteran. "Walter the Educator" shares his time between educating and creating. He holds interests and owns several creative projects that entertain, enlighten, enhance, and educate, hoping to inspire and motivate you. Follow, find new works, and stay up to date with Walter the Educator™

at WaltertheEducator.com

www.ingramcontent.com/pod-product-compliance
Lightning Source LLC
LaVergne TN
LVHW012050070526
838201LV00082B/3894